Tunnel of Light and Dark

Holly Ziemba

Copyright © 2021 by Holly Ziemba.

Library of Congress Control Number: 2021914658
ISBN: Hardcover 978-1-6641-8600-2
Softcover 978-1-6641-8599-9
eBook 978-1-6641-8598-2

All rights reserved. No part of this book may be reproduced or transmitted in any form or by any means, electronic or mechanical, including photocopying, recording, or by any information storage and retrieval system, without permission in writing from the copyright owner.

Any people depicted in stock imagery provided by Getty Images are models, and such images are being used for illustrative purposes only.
Certain stock imagery © Getty Images.

Print information available on the last page.

Rev. date: 07/19/2021

To order additional copies of this book, contact:
Xlibris
844-714-8691
www.Xlibris.com
Orders@Xlibris.com
828057

Contents

The Van 1
The Little Things 2
I Succeed 3
Relationships 4
Grandpa, I Love You 5
I Will For You 6
Miss the Old Times 7
Too Much 8
Who? 9
On Her Own 10
Miss 11
Note to Self 12
I Wouldn't Have Gone 13
Say It Loud 15
A Very Long Time Ago 16
I Did Not Pass Your Test 17
So Many Times 18
Dark to Light 19
Lesson Learned 20
Him 21
One Kiss Is Not So Simple 22
Friday the 6th, 2008 23
I See Her 24
The Proposal 25
Close to You 26
Today Is Love 27
Time Stands Still 28
No Love in That 29
Like Magnets 30
Another Generation 31
A Year's Worth of Moments 32
If We Could Rewind Time, Would It Change Anything? 33
11/5/2011 34

20412	35
One Road Away	36
The One That Got Away	37
Still Standing	38
Easier to Forget You	39
Untitled	40
I Truly Love You	41
I See Your Light	42
Lake Michigan Evening	43
Through Her Memory	44
You	45
I Have Faith in You	46
Not the Same	47
Do You See Me?	48
Grandma, I Miss You	49
Creating Myself	50

Tunnel of Light and Dark

The Van

I rode home on my bike, and the fall air chilled me
I stopped to button my jacket and could feel him looking at me
The van on the side of the road with the engine off

The man pretended to sleep, when I looked his way
I felt the tightness in my chest as I pedaled away
The van on the side of the road with the engine on

I didn't know what way to take, but rode as fast as I could
I couldn't believe this was happening to me in my own neighborhood
The van and the man, no time to stop for help

I was going so fast, but he was gaining on me
No matter how hard I pedaled, he was just behind me
The van didn't slow, but neither did I

Just a couple more houses, and I hit the safe zone
I jumped off my bike and ran into my home
The van, the blue van, with the orange ladder
He almost got caught me, but I was faster

The Little Things

A handshake to greet
A nod to say hi
A smile for how are you
A wave for goodbye

A call to catch up
A hug says I miss you
A wink for precious moments
A kiss for feeling true

A card to remind that you didn't forget
A cuddle to show you care
A flower for special times
An appearance to say you'll be there

I Succeed

I live
Love
Learn
I succeed

I care
Trust
Dream
I succeed

I run
Jump
Leap life's hurdles
I succeed

I hope
Believe
Never give up
I succeed

Relationships

Gentle love
Gentle hug
No lies

Gentle hands
Gentle touch
Caring eyes

Harsh words
Last kiss
Hard goodbyes

Heartaches
Bad pains
Many cries

Grandpa, I Love You

Please don't leave me
It's not time for you to go
I love you so much
I just wanted you to know

I'm still young
So are you
Seeing the IV's tangled
My nightmare is coming true

You make me laugh
Seeing you helpless makes me cry
I pray for a miracle
I don't want to say goodbye

You say you'll see me in the funny papers
You tell me to smile
I don't want to face the truth
Stay with me a while

I can't imagine life without you
I need you to be there
It's not your turn
No one knows how much I care

I hold your hand
You're so cold
My tears fall
I want you to see me grow old

I sit still
There is nothing I can do
Don't close your eyes
Grandpa, I love you

I Will For You

I will hold you
Be there
Kiss you
Care

I will understand
Not hold back
Listen
Keep on track

I will be honest
Tell you all I know
Hold you tight
Never let go

I will look you in the eyes
Show you how I feel
Give you all I have
Always be real

I will remember the good times
Be your friend
Keep my faith
Stay until the end

I will be strong
Trust you
Stick by your side
Love you

Miss the Old Times

I miss the times we spent together skating on the ice
You looked me in the eyes
I miss the times we held onto hands
You hurt me when you told lies

I miss the long talks on the phone
You always made me laugh
I miss the way you kissed me
Until we headed down the wrong path

I miss our friendship
My heart became your toy
I miss how you tried to act like a man
You were only just a boy

I don't miss the way you played me
Or every moment I felt sad
Though we did not make it
I still miss what we had

Too Much

I trembled
I cried
My stomach was in knots
My heart was in pain
I swore I wouldn't let it happen again
I got back on my feet
I stayed grounded
I thought it was love I had lost
Though it was never love to begin with

Who?

Who is he?

Who will love me for more than just a while?
Who will hold my hand and make me smile?

Who will make me laugh and hate to see me cry?
Who will like me for me and never say goodbye?

Who will be there for me, when there is nowhere else to turn?
Who will always love me, not just out of concern?

Who will care for me when I am sick?
Who will be there for me through thin and thick?

Who will be there through the good and bad?
Who will mend my heart when I am feeling sad?

Who will hold me close and never let me go?
Who will tell me they love me, not just assume I know?

Who will take me to the sunset and walk along the pier?
Who will be sweet and kind?
Who will be sincere?

On Her Own

On her own
She raised her kids
She held down a job
She paid the bills

On her own
She managed
She always did her best
She took on much
She became depressed

On her own
She learned from her mistakes
She took life one day at a time
She did it
She found love in herself

Miss

Miss the frosties and the times we shared
The wild bull rides and when we cared

Miss the hugs and the kisses too
The drives to church and miss you

Miss the tickles and the camping
The family game nights and the laughing

Miss you and not her
Miss the love
Miss my father

Note to Self

Ms. Young-and-Innocent
You have no idea what's in store
Get mad a little less
Smile a little more

Ms. Independent
You're on track to be alone
Loosen up control
Let your soul be shown

Ms. Defensive
Learn to calm your reply
It doesn't look good on you
The rolling of your eyes

Ms. Critical
Not every path can be yours
A few open windows
A few closed doors

Ms. Perfection
You're not going to reach it
Don't beat yourself up
Perfection is not realistic

Ms. Optimistic
There's so much you can do
Believe in yourself
Even when it's hard to

I Wouldn't Have Gone

It was a beautiful night
Everyone dressed to the nines
Music and dancing
The night was mine

When I think back
I can't remember him there
Maybe he wasn't so significant
Or I was trying not to care

The night slowed as did the dance
But the after was to come
If I knew then what I know now
I wouldn't have gone

The drinks went down fast
I became messy
In the back seat of a car
I can't remember undressing

I could feel the pain
But my body was numb
I remember the lights
And laughter from some

The night air hit my face
As I crawled out of the car
Another cliché prom night
Had gone too far

I didn't want to go back
A teacher threatened to spread the news
The more stories spread around school
The more I felt bruised

I didn't want this
I wanted to be sober and choose
But I can't just blame him
Because he was young and drunk too

Say It Loud

Hey, pretty girl, don't cry
High school will soon be out of sight

Don't marinate in the mistakes you have made
Everything will be all right

Take it from me, who knows you best
I know all of your hidden secrets

You're better than this, don't judge yourself
Try not to show your weakness

You'll learn the curve, as it had to happen
For you to discover your path

Seek forgiveness with the one above
Don't spotlight your wrath

Find a little faith
Push away each cloud

Take control and find your voice
Say it loud

A Very Long Time Ago

I pulled up and waited for you
Didn't think it would go that far
You opened my door and sat down next to me
And pretended it was just another talk
You gave me the right to choose
I could not choose you
Not because I didn't want to
But because I knew it wouldn't last
You closed the door behind you
I wanted to grab your hand
I wanted to call your name, but I didn't
I heard your engine start
I wanted to call and tell you to stop
I wanted to say I would choose you
But I let you drive away
You turned the corner, and I believed you were gone forever
I cried with my head down on my steering wheel
My heart was shattered
Thank God for unanswered prayers

I Did Not Pass Your Test

Our relationship was on fire from the very start
Our fire burned bright
You were the match, and I was the light

It all seemed perfect on the surface
Our story line was simple
Until your actions became fickle

Simon says stop, Simon says go
You had me in the palm of your hands
We were blowing away like shifting sands

You pushed my door back open when I was just about to lock it
I was reminded I was not in control
You never cared how much you stole

You were like fresh air I took in at the beach
But I saw it happen again
Your bitter taste at every end

I let you control me the way you wanted
Until I let you wash away with the rain
I belong to me, and I am no longer yours to claim

So Many Times

Today I sit alone
Tomorrow I do the same
Pointing fingers
Finding someone to blame

I do not want to feel like this
Why am I this way?
Leaving my body
Nothing to say

Feeling so enclosed
My heart dies slowly
Pouring through my skin
Pushing until I am lonely

Torn from start to finish
Everything to perish
I want to give it all away
Saving nothing to cherish

Wishing for the end
When it fades away
Leaving me breathless
Nothing to say

Down is where I am
No time for me to spare
Pushing rewind
I don't want to care

Dark to Light

I walk through the dark at a slow pace

Sometimes it felt thrilling and at times depressing

There were moments I wasn't scared and moments of fear

I embraced the dark as it came naturally with the pills

There was always light inside of me, but the shadows kept it hidden

Who had I turned into as I made my way through

I could not recognize who I had become

So I opened my eyes and read my own words

My words were a mirror that forced me to look deep

I didn't like what I saw, but knew I was still in there

There was still time and hope that the path could be brighter

More determination and self-realization than ever

All it took was a glimmer to get me running

I ran through the dark to the light at the end of my tunnel

Lesson Learned

I smile when I think of you because you used to make me laugh
I laugh now that you're alone because of your wicked ways
Love, it was never that kind of love
Like the love that I have now
You insist because you like the control
But this girl knows those tricks
I wish you happiness
But have yet to see you find it
You may find what I have found
But only if you change

Him

So nervous
So flustered
Time ticks
My heart beats

So breathless
So scared
Chills rush
My heart pounds

So anxious
So serious
Thoughts spiral
My heart races

So happy
So shaken
Can't wait
My heart flutters

One Kiss Is Not So Simple

One kiss against my lips could mean a change forever
One kiss for change is all you want to know
One kiss could be the last time I see you
One kiss might be an adventure
One kiss I wish to push away
One kiss I think about as I lay my head to rest
One kiss at the wrong time could be ever so sweet
One kiss I cannot let you have
One kiss brings back all the good and bad
One kiss avoided with the turn of my cheek
One kiss not meant to share
One kiss I want to share with the one I truly love
One kiss is not so simple
One kiss against my lips could mean a change forever

Friday the 6th, 2008

The wind swirled through past tense
The storm raged and displaced things that were not its own
The flower held tight through its roots in fear of losing its petals
Raindrops held heavy on the leaves as the storm blew through
The storm passed
The flower stood strong
Though not as tall
She stood taller

I See Her

The little girl from the trailer park
Wondered her worth at times
Some people may have looked down
But she stood as tall as the trees

Her feet took her to her destination
Her heart took her there with passion
She had the potential
To accomplish everything

The girl with the trials
Like every other girl
We were all the same
Just trying to get by

The woman who lifted herself
She lifted others too
She knew in her heart
The mission she was on

The fire was inside
She lit the match
Déjà vu reminded her she was on the right track
Nothing was going to stop her

The Proposal

The cool air laid across our laps
We sat in his grandparent's old swing
I never thought it would be that night
He was down on one knee
There were tears in his eyes when he looked up at me
I could feel it in my heart
He asked me to be his forever
I couldn't imagine anything else
I know we were meant for each other

Close to You

I don't need much more than cool night air
Or raindrops on a tin roof
A hug and kiss become a habit
I want to cherish each one as if it were our last
I don't need much more than a man on one knee
Or the chilling sound of thunder
How beautiful it is waking up next to you
If I could only freeze our moments

Today Is Love

Love is two hearts that beat as one
It's the happiness every day
It's the way we look at each other

Love is respect and a bond
It's the hugs and kisses at night
It's the trials two can overcome

Love is the exchanging of vows
It's the beauty seen in each other
Today is love

Time Stands Still

The precious memories
And the pictures
Remind me every single day

The holiday dinners
The remembrance ornaments
Remind me it's been a short time

The hugs
And the tears
Remind me I am not that strong

The thoughts
And the spiraling
Remind me the sadness lasts forever

The dreams
And the feelings
Reminds me I can't stop believing you're there

Time stands still

No Love in That

There is no love in the letter you wrote
Or the way you just drive by

There is no love in the home you live
Or how you ask me why

There is no love in the battle we fought
Or the time we've spent apart

There is no love in the way your stories change
Or the chance for a new start

There is no love in the last ten years
Or when you shared my letter

There is no love in the way I feel
Or your promise to make it better

Like Magnets

You caught me when I wasn't ready
I was already yours
Before I was yours

I clung like a magnet
I tried to pull away
But your strength was unmatchable

The strings began to unravel
We were losing grip
Love wasn't enough

We filled the voids
We pretended
The hurt was layers deep

You pulled me back in
It was a trap I learned quick
I couldn't take it again

We filled the voids
We pretended
The hurt was layers deep

We locked eyes, but I was angry
Your heart was open
I wanted to run

I stayed for a second back in your arms
The comfort reassured
Just like that, you drew me back in

We clung like a magnet
We didn't pull away
We created a beautiful life

Another Generation

The first day I held on to you, changed my life forever
When I saw the look in her eyes, I could tell it changed her too
No song could capture everything precious about you
You cannot fake love that grasps every string of your heart
Every moment has melted my heart a little more
There is nothing I would not do for you
I cannot look at you without seeing her smile
I hope you take on all the qualities that we love about your mother

A Year's Worth of Moments

You stand as tall as the others, but you're special
I take a picture of you to freeze the moment
To capture the seasons as they pass
Today you are glowing in the sun and so many shades of green
You turn vibrant and colorful, as if a rainbow crashed upon your leaves
You will lose those many shades and be stripped down to your bare
You will turn cold and hold weight that is not your own
But you will hold that weight beautifully
By your many changes, we are reminded that another year has passed

If We Could Rewind Time, Would It Change Anything?

I sometimes wish you loved me like the song "I Loved Her First"

That song we danced to on my wedding day

If I could live that over again, I would, even if it broke my heart

I see myself in you sometimes, but learned my values from her

She is the one who has always been there

I wish you were always there too

The pain I write on this paper is from the sadness
over the past fourteen years

You would think I would be over it, but it's just below the surface

We pass each other in our cars and don't even turn our heads

You said you would make an effort, so why didn't you?

I'll ask myself that question for the rest of my life

11/5/2011

I felt the lump in my throat all day
I knew he felt it too
You were taken from us
Taken away too soon
We talked of stories old and new
Stories made us feel all right
Our tears watered the soil around you
While we stood under the moonlight
I know you were there
It meant a lot everyone
I cannot wrap my head around it
Knowing you are forever gone
I wish I could take the pain away from your brother
But I sit here feeling it too
We will miss you for the rest of our lives
We will honor you

20412

I went there to say hi to my grandpa and found a grandpa I never knew
I took a few more steps and found my cousins too

There is something about visiting them that made me appreciate life
The cool air and the sun on my skin reminded me I'd be okay

The trees in my front yard change as the seasons do
The seasons pass, and my hands wrinkle too

I cast my cares each night
I can feel him strengthen me

Just one prayer away
He's there for me

One Road Away

Don't give me the satisfaction of "I'm sorry"

The pit in my stomach tightens when I hear your words in my head

I know you feel that same pit when you open the front door

All I need is time to forget you

Yet I still wish I could fix it

But there are many things I would selfishly wish for first

Why did you allow this to happen to us?

Your eyes are open, but your vision is blurry

Does your bed feel empty? How about your heart?

The feeling of family, I hope you feel again

But I will not wish for it

Because there are many things I would selfishly wish for first

The One That Got Away

Just before dusk, I walked the pier alone
No cares and no overthinking
The ice on the lake floated so peacefully
No worries until the adrenaline rushed
I just wanted the shot before the sunset
No one around but the man far back
I could feel in my body, he was no good
Nowhere to go but back to cross his path
On the phone, with a battery almost dead
I saw evil in his eyes as he passed
I could feel the darkness in him
Please don't turn back, don't turn back my way
I hung up the phone so I could run, but he started to gain speed
No one to help me, so I found comfort in prayer
I made it just before he got to me
I sped down the winding roads
Not sure I would find safety
Until my love was in view

Still Standing

My armor has weathered
Insides deteriorate
Windows wide open
You can see right through
Moments chipped away little parts of me
My voice travels in echo's
Echo's that pass through the room
One wrong move
The walls could cave in
I'm finding beauty in my perish
The dust begins to settle
I make my way back
Wearing these shoes that fit
Still standing

Easier to Forget You

I want to hurt you back
That's what you have done to me
I want to text you one more time
I guess I'll let it be

You would think I would be smarter
Learn to stay away
It would be easier to forget you
If you weren't one road away

Your conspiracy theories
Her wicked grin
Write us one more letter
Tell us how we've sinned

Remember when we were young
She told us we had to knock
There goes another year
Too late to rewind the clock

It's normal not to have you here
It's been this way for years
I hate that this is out of my control
And that I allow these tears

I'm glad to see you try as a grandpa
But miss the dad you tried to be
Lock me out and push me away again
Throw away the key

Untitled

This home does not feel like a home today
I am just here
I never thought words could hurt so badly
I was clearly wrong
You're only a few steps away
Our connection is miles apart
I look outside at the beautiful day
I wish I could feel that warmth
It's hard to find forgiveness

I Truly Love You

I love that you don't let me win every fight
But you do sometimes
I love laughing at you when you've drunk too much
And when you roll around the living room floor with the dogs
I love that you still order pizza for two, just the way I like
Even when I say I'm not hungry
I love that you still open my door
No matter the weather
I love that you weren't just a one-night stand
Because I wanted to keep you
I love your flaws and your perfections
Even though your flaws frustrate me at times
I love you for everything you love about me
And that you forgive me for my weaknesses
I truly love you

I See Your Light

I see you start to come around
You're trying harder with them
I felt like there was nothing to make you want me
But that's my own insecurities
I'm not sure what has changed, but I'm starting to see it
It seems there is a weight lifted
Your smile is making its way back
I hear your laughter too
I see your effort
I see part of your heart
We talk about how life is short
We ride bikes into the sunset
I'm not expecting it to last, but it's good to have you near
Please stay
Keep building
I see your light

Lake Michigan Evening

Water rushes
Tall grass sways
Cool air passes through my window

Waves crash over the pier
People walk about
I close my eyes to take in the sound

The sky holds gray
Birds fly away
I find peace in these moments

Through Her Memory

The hourglass is filling
The clock is ticking
I'm trying to grab hold

Our little's are growing
The sun is rising
Winter is clearing again

The calendar pages are turning
The sun is setting
Summer is on the horizon

My hands are aging
My skin is weathering
I'm missing moments I can never get back

My mind is forgetting
My children are worrying
Where have the last five years gone?

My memory is stuck
My body is crippling
There's nothing we can do to control it

My eyes are open
But my light is dimming
It's only a matter of time
Until the last grain of sand falls

You

When my tears fall
I call on you
When I have nowhere to turn
It's you I turn to
When my health is declining
I call on you
When I have taken on too much
You're there to take it on too
When I am proud of my accomplishments
I call on you
When my worries get the best of me
You say there's nothing I can't do
When I think about my life
The person to thank is you
When you need me
I'll be there for you too

I Have Faith in You

Put it down
You don't need it
You don't need to be numb
Just find your confidence

Tip the bottle over
Let it drain
You're better than the number of drinks you've had
I have faith in you

Feel the sober
Let it free you
Clear the negative thoughts
We need you back

Detach and find peace
Take a deep breath
Let your heart mend
You have what it takes

Not the Same

I am not the same girl that I was years ago
I have power at my fingertips
I am not afraid to try
I am not afraid to fail while trying
I will not be held back
I know my worth
I value my time
I am not consumed by my past
I do not have to control it all
I am beautiful
I am worth it
I am
Me.

Do You See Me?

I see you for all that you are
You are trying to do better
I've seen your harshness after my bitter words
Our chapters have not been easy

I see your light flicker
You try as much as you know how
I see the distance, and I understand it
The hurt doesn't fade completely

I see more confidence in you
Yes, you have made mistakes
But there's a chance for redemption
We can fix the future together

I see you
Do you see me?

Grandma, I Miss You

My chest gets heavy
The raw feelings start to show
Grandma, I miss you so much
I am sure you already know

I wanted to be there with you
They wouldn't let me
Just to see your face
You still remembered me

A memory showed up
I was there just last year
We painted spring colors
Now I look at them with tears

You were frail when I last left you
I was angry and hurt
I wanted to hug you and pretend you'd be okay
But they lowered you into the dirt

All my childhood memories flood
The one's when time stood still
Buckets of rainwater
Tomatoes in the window sill

Your gentle hands
And your porcelain skin
Your funny little smirk
And everywhere we've been

Time was stolen away
Just one more walk through the door
A quiet "Hi, honey"
I wish to hear once more

Creating Myself

I've felt hopeless and torn
Like I was losing grip
I've felt weighted and heavy
With barely a sign of struggle

I've felt trapped and overtaken
Lost and confused
I've felt self-conscious and unworthy
I've been my own worst critic

I feel strong and independent
Motivated to shine
I feel powerful and brave
I've changed my state of mind

I feel light, and I feel free
Like the wind blowing through my hair
I feel serious and determined
No one can slow this train

I feel focused and worthy
Less pressure for perfection
I feel passionate and empowered
Taking the path less traveled

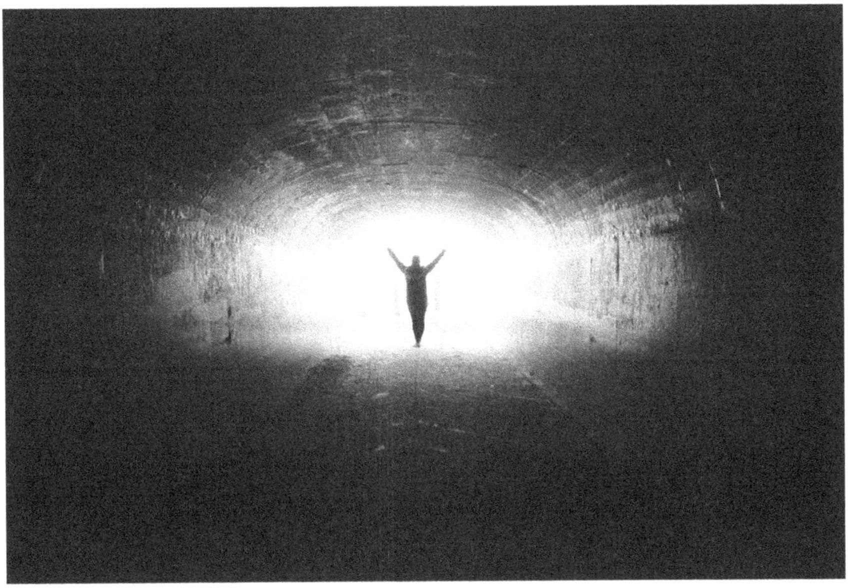

Index

A

A handshake to greet 2

D

Don't give me the satisfaction of "I'm sorry" 36

G

Gentle love 4

H

Hey, pretty girl, don't cry 15

I

I am not the same girl that I was years ago 47
I don't need much more than cool night air 26
I felt the lump in my throat all day 34
I love that you don't let me win every fight 41
I miss the times we spent together skating on the ice 7
I pulled up and waited for you 16
I rode home on my bike, and the fall air chilled me 1
I see you for all that you are
I see you start to come around
I smile when I think of you because you used to make me laugh 20
I sometimes wish you loved me like the song "I Loved Her First" 33
I trembled 8
I walk through the dark at a slow pace 19
I want to hurt you back 39
I went there to say hi to my grandpa and found a grandpa I never knew 35
I will hold you 6
It was a beautiful night 13
I've felt hopeless and torn 50

J

Just before dusk, I walked the pier alone 37

L

Love is two hearts that beat as one 27

M

Ms. Young-and-Innocent 12
My armor has weathered 38
My chest gets heavy 49

O

On her own 10
One kiss against my lips could mean a change forever 22
Our relationship was on fire from the very start 17

P

Please don't leave me 5
Put it down 46

S

So nervous 21

T

The cool air laid across our laps 25
The first day I held on to you, changed my life forever 31
The hourglass is filling 44
The little girl from the trailer park 24
The precious memories 28
There is no love in the letter you wrote 29
The wind swirled through past tense 23

This home does not feel like a home today 40

W

Water rushes 43
When my tears fall 45
Who is he? 9

Y

You caught me when I wasn't ready 30
You stand as tall as the others, but you're special 32